MATTHEW DIGBY WYATT

MATTHEW DIGBY WYATT

THE FIRST CAMBRIDGE
SLADE PROFESSOR OF FINE ART

An Inaugural Lecture
by

NIKOLAUS PEVSNER

CAMBRIDGE
AT THE UNIVERSITY PRESS
1950

CAMBRIDGE UNIVERSITY PRESS
Cambridge, New York, Melbourne, Madrid, Cape Town, Singapore,
São Paulo, Delhi, Dubai, Tokyo, Mexico City

Cambridge University Press
The Edinburgh Building, Cambridge CB2 8RU, UK

Published in the United States of America by Cambridge University Press, New York

www.cambridge.org
Information on this title: www.cambridge.org/9780521170765

First published 1950
First paperback edition 2010

A catalogue record for this publication is available from the British Library

ISBN 978-0-521-17076-5 Paperback

Dedicated to the
Royal Institute of British Architects
and its
Library Staff

but for whose help
the preparation of this lecture would not
have been possible

CONTENTS

LIST OF PLATES
(AT END)

ACKNOWLEDGMENTS

FOR help received I wish to thank Miss Lore Strich who took the photograph for me from which Plate VI is made; the Librarians of Ealing, Kensington, Lambeth and the Guildhall (City of London); Mrs Warmington of Flowerdown Cottage, Littleton, nr. Winchester; and Major Painter of the Essex Regiment, Warley Barracks, Brentwood, Essex.

N. P.

February 1950

THE LECTURE

Mr Vice-Chancellor, Ladies and Gentlemen,
'In addressing you for the first time from this chair it is natural that I should feel a certain amount of embarrassing emotions.' These words, you will agree, are a very proper beginning for an inaugural lecture. But they are not mine. They are Sir Matthew Digby Wyatt's, the first sentence of his inaugural lecture, when he had been made Slade Professor of Fine Art in 1869. At about the same time Ruskin had become Slade Professor at Oxford. Ruskin was—I suppose one would have to say—an author and journalist. Wyatt was an architect, a member of a family which has pro-duced at least nine other architects, and among them such ornaments of the profession as James Wyatt of Fonthill, Ashridge and the Pantheon in Oxford Street, Jeffry of Sidney Sussex College and the Gothic modernization of Windsor, and Thomas Henry, Matthew Digby's brother, whose Wilton church of 1844 was one of the most famous examples of a revived Early Christian style.

Matthew Digby has not designed anything quite so prominent, and the aesthetic quality of his

1

buildings is distressing indeed, as I shall have occasion to show. But he was a successful man, though more in administration and organization than in art: Honorary Secretary to the Royal Institute of British Architects from 1855 to 1859, Gold Medallist and Vice-President of the R.I.B.A., Hon. M.A. Cambridge, Knight of the Legion of Honour, and so on.

He was forty-nine when he was elected to the newly founded Slade professorship, on the strength of his writings no doubt more than his buildings.[1] He had been articled to his brother Thomas Henry, who was thirteen years his elder, and had then, as was almost *de rigueur* amongst architects at that time, travelled on the Continent and published the results of his journeys. His chief interest had been the adornment of church interiors, an interest aroused no doubt by his brother, who had, when Matthew started on his travels, just completed the much-discussed and much-praised decoration in mosaic of Wilton church. So Matthew's first publication was *Specimens of the Geometrical Mosaic of the Middle Ages*. It came out in 1848, and was followed later by others on polychromy in decoration, on metalwork, textile art, and the applied arts in general (see Appendix A).

The next year, 1849, was decisive in Wyatt's career. The Society of Arts commissioned him to write a report on an exhibition of French industrial products held in Paris. He went over with Henry Cole and thus won the friendship of a most remarkable Victorian.[2] Cole was a civil servant but had also busied himself in the course of the late 'thirties and early 'forties with propaganda for penny postage and a wide railway gauge, with the creation of the Grimsby Docks and with the designing and publishing of children's books, of the first Christmas card ever printed, and of pictorial railway charts to acquaint passengers with the sights their train was passing. He also designed and sold through a shop what he called art manufactures, that is objects in pottery, glass, silver, etc., which were meant to be exemplary in design. He joined the Society of Arts in 1846, three years after Prince Albert had accepted the Society's presidency. The two men, equal in 'indomitable energy and perseverance', to use your William Whewell's words,[3] got on splendidly, and one result of their co-operation was the Great Exhibition of the Industrial Products of All Nations which, when it opened on 1 May 1851, was the first international exhibition ever held anywhere.

Its spiritual originator was Cole, and his journey to Paris with young Wyatt was part of his campaign to convince, first Albert and then all England, of the glories and advantages of a London exhibition such as he dreamt it.

He visualized a vast building displaying everything from raw materials and machinery to works of sculpture. But art applied to industry, which term incidentally was first introduced by Albert,[4] was going to be the backbone of the show. And there Cole and his friends cannot have been quite so certain of glories to come or even of a very large number of adequate exhibits.

For Cole and his friends—a small band comprising such notable men as Owen Jones, the architect, author of that famous book, *The Grammar of Ornament*, which was last reprinted in 1928, and of a monumental folio on the Alhambra, William Dyce, the Scottish Nazarene and pre-Pre-Raphaelite, Richard Redgrave another painter, later to be Inspector General of Art, and no doubt, although we have not much in the way of proof, Gottfried Semper, the great German architect, who at the time was a political refugee in England[5]—this small band was highly critical of the state of industrial art in England, even before the Exhibition of 1851 had shown of what atrocities the Early Victorian Age was capable.

We know now pretty well how this disintegration of design had come about in the decades before 1850. The reshuffling of society which was the inevitable outcome of the industrial revolution had brought up to the top a class of people who had not enjoyed the aesthetic training of the Age of Taste nor had the leisure to acquire aesthetic appreciation in later life. Hence we find in painting the success of the anecdotic—Landseer's *High Life and Low Life*, Leslie's *My Uncle Toby and Widow Wadman*—and the withdrawal from a public life of all those painters who wished to pursue more aesthetically relevant problems. They made less and less efforts to please the public— a public indeed less and less worth pleasing—and concentrated on unalloyed aesthetic subtleties. Art for art's sake in its turn made their possibilities of social acceptance less likely, and so the vicious circle was complete. You know of the insults to which the young Pre-Raphaelites, the young Impressionists and Whistler were exposed and conversely of their scorn for the public.

But while a painter, just like a composer, can create in the solitude of his attic, and can at least keep up a self-delusion of independence of the public (hence the highest achievements in nineteenth-century art are achievements of music and painting);[6] a designer for industry and an architect cannot. That difference explains what was happening to architecture and design during the Victorian Age. A house or a sideboard does not take place unless it pleases a layman or a number of laymen, be they client or manufacturer or buyer. And what pleased them about 1850? Certainly not what was subtle, because to appreciate subtlety in proportion, outline, etc., requires training and leisure. So effects had to be loud, and if appreciation could be conducted along lines of *literary association* rather than purely aesthetic exposition—so much the better. Hence the insistence of nineteenth-century architecture on the imitation of styles of the past. Different styles of the past are more easily recognized than different moods expressed by the abstract means of design within one and the same style. Also the archaeological knowledge which an architect could display in imitating the Romanesque of Lombardy or the Third Pointed of East Anglia was a provable, as it were a scientific quality, and thus accessible to the nineteenth-century patron. And, besides, why a college should look Gothic, the Athenaeum Club Grecian, a club of liberal merchants and their champions Florentine Renaissance, and a rich man's London mansion like a super *hôtel particulier* in Paris, could also be understood without straining one's aesthetic perceptions.

Matthew Digby Wyatt's own buildings (see Appendix B) are a case in point, and so it might be worth while looking at some of them. Amongst his earliest architectural designs is what he did for the Crystal Palace at the time of its re-erection at Sydenham, that is in 1854. The Byzantine Court we know in a state of ideal freshness from a water-colour at the Victoria and Albert Museum (Plate II). It is quite enjoyable as a water-colour,[7] painted in hot colours under a smiling blue sky, with fat dark green and *sang-de-bœuf* columns and a general rotundity characteristic of the mid-nineteenth century. There is not much fantasy in the design itself, no doubt because of the educational purpose of the structure. As for the Byzantine style one must, of course, not take this as in any way representing a personal predilection of Wyatt. He also designed for the Crystal Palace the Pompeian, English Gothic, French Gothic, Elizabethan, Italian Renaissance and some other Courts and Vestibules.

While this catholic assortment of styles introduces us to Wyatt the architectural scholar and the future professor, we can see him at Paddington Station, also in 1854, taking time off as it were to enjoy himself (Plate V, *b*). The ground-floor of the central feature of Platform One, with the Queen's apartment behind, is vaguely of the French Dix-huitième, while on the upper floor two Quattroccento windows flank a debased Palladian or Venetian window. There is in addition plenty of incised and fretwork ornament all along the platform, and at the old south end of the station too. It is all very jolly in a ham-fisted way, as near as our Wyatt ever got to the style of the Victorian music-hall, that is the folk-art or popular art of the nineteenth century. It has—no doubt deliberately—none of the classical gravity and discipline of Hardwick's Euston Station. In fact the most striking feature of Wyatt's work at Paddington is the lack of self-discipline, the relief at being for a change off one's best behaviour, the relief at relaxation. One must examine the whole building to get the flavour of this completely relaxed tensionless trailing on of ornament. One consequence of this brief abandon of best behaviour is that Paddington is emphatically not period imitation. That makes it so particularly important for an understanding of Wyatt's own taste.

We find the same weakly flamboyance appearing more timidly in the Royal Engineers' Crimean War Memorial at Chatham (Plate V, *a*). The design is in adapted Italian Renaissance forms with the addition of a few original decorative bits, such as the volutes. The arch was erected in 1861. In 1862 Wyatt did one design for the Albert Memorial as a classical temple and another as an Italian Gothic Cross. I don't know what they looked like, but I do know that in the same year, for an office building in Grafton Street, Dublin (Plate III, a), he chose the Italian style of the fourteenth century.[8] Again certain details, such as the shop windows below and the attic story with its stumpy piers above, are deliberately incorrect, that is, mark a conscious or unconscious improvement by the Victorian architect on his Trecento predecessors. And it is quite obvious that they succeed in making the building look High Victorian. If one tries to analyse what else is here specifically High Victorian, I would point to three qualities. First, the all-over covering of the whole façade with motifs, second, the fact that all the motifs used are rather rich and robust, and third, the lack of any resolute accents. This general even pitch of oratory is especially characteristic. The eighteen-thirties and 'forties still believed in contrasts of emphasized and unemphasized parts, though obviously not as much as the Georgians. That is evident, for instance, to use Cambridge examples, in the Fitzwilliam Museum by Basevi and Cockerell which was begun in 1837. The coming men in the eighteen-seventies believed in accents again, as you can see in Waterhouse's work at Girton (begun in 1873) and Champneys's at Newnham (begun in 1875).

After Wyatt's Tuscan Gothic, some Genoese Cinquecento of his!—The job this time was a government building, the courtyard of Gilbert Scott's India Office in Whitehall (Plate III, *b*). So Wyatt was more restrained, but he did not give up what splendour he regarded as appropriate. The detail is uncommonly carefully designed, and the effect undeniably one of festive public display.

In the case of private display, Wyatt felt considerably less inhibited. For the Salon at Ashridge (1864), for instance, he designed huge doorways in aedicule surrounds with heavy broken segmental pediments and fireplaces supported by life-size labouring caryatids. Even more Gargantuan was the fireplace in the Hall of Clare College, Cambridge, redecorated by Wyatt in 1870–2. Willis and Clark tell us that it cost £3500 and was 'ornamented with large oak figures, supporting a bust of the foundress, the woodwork enriched with arabesques and festoons'. The plaster ceiling hung from iron girders is still *in situ* though regrettably simplified.

The odd combination of the festive with the turgid which characterizes these fireplaces, is also exhibited in Wyatt's mausoleum for Eveline Rothschild at the Jewish Cemetery, West Ham. Mrs Rothschild died young in 1866. The mausoleum (Plate VI) is circular with a dome of eighteenth-century detail on attached Corinthian columns. The panels between the columns with

10

their naturalistic flower motifs in the centres and the ornamental ironwork above the panels deserve the attention of the student of mid-Victorian detail.

Alford House, Kensington (Plate IV, *a*) is also classical, but this time with an admixture of the Parisian of Henri IV. The French roof is unmistakable. However, the red brick, the swags and the setting transfer one's thoughts from France to England and in particular Christopher Wren's England.

Purely English, but in the Tudor style, is Wyatt's most spectacular country mansion, Possingworth Manor built for Mr Huth, the celebrated collector. The design is of the accepted asymmetry, with decoration even extending into the roof—Wyatt had himself designed ornamental roof-tiles in several colours for a manufacturer. The Gothic version of the Venetian window in the middle gable should be specially noted. A similar carefree confusion of motifs reigns supreme in the Hall of Possingworth. The fireplace is Gothic, the ceiling Jacobean, the upholstery in its unmistakably bulgy curves Victorian and nothing else. But again the essential feature is the all-over covering of everything from floor to ceiling with ornament of some sort, a monotonous process without emphases or punctuation.

11

Nowhere else in Wyatt's *œuvre* does this embarrassing lack of concentration come out more distressingly than in Addenbrooke's Hospital at Cambridge of 1864 (Plate IV, *b*). It is sufficient to look at these symmetrical wings with their buttresses holding up an arcade with closely set columns, and the two broader arcades with a third above displaying a kind of weak Gothic lintels which connect the wings with a weakly recessed Tudor centre, and one cannot fail to feel that deliberation must have dictated to the architect this covering of his whole surface with whatever motifs, but that the quality and juxtaposition of these motifs shows him to have been a highly insensitive architect.

Surely it would be perverse to exhume Wyatt on the occasion of so special a lecture, if there were nothing to him but this display of architectural thick-skinnedness. In fact, however, his buildings are no more than a foil to his achievement in other fields. He was first of all Secretary to the Executive Committee for the 1851 Exhibition, an excellent appointment not only for his administrative abilities, but also because he was an uncannily clear-sighted critic and theorist of design and architecture.

To give one early example, he wrote in 1850 apropos design in ironwork that no successful results can be attained...until either 1st the manufacturer and designer are one individual doubly gifted, or 2nd the manufacturer takes the pains to investigate and master so much of the elements of design as shall at least enable him to judiciously control the artist; or 3rd the artist by a careful study of the material and its manufacture shall elaborate and employ a system of design in harmony with, and special to, the peculiarities so evolved.

This passage comes from an article published in the *Journal of Design and Manufactures*,[9] a short-lived but very noteworthy magazine conceived also originally by Cole, and edited by Richard Redgrave.[10] The leading members of the circle of the *Journal of Design* were all a good deal older than Wyatt,[11] but he picked up their favourite theses in no time, and they were indeed novel, daring and convincing enough.[12]

It is generally assumed that the reformatory reaction against the atrocities of Early Victorian decorative art began with William Morris, and I have perhaps myself helped to perpetuate this fallacy.[13] But William Morris's lectures began only in 1877, and here are a few passages from the *Journal of Design*—which came out from 1849 to 1852—and from some other early writings of its contributors. I want to quote them at some length, not only because they seem to have so much in

13

common with Morris, but also because they sound so remarkably topical even to-day, especially in surroundings in which it is not in the least yet an axiom that new buildings should be designed and furnished in a contemporary style.

'Chaos and disorder' rule in art to-day.[14] 'Everyone elects his own style.... We all agree only in being wretched imitators.'[15] 'Our best things are more or less faithful reminiscences.'[16] Yet it must obviously remain a 'vain and foolish attempt to make the art which faithfully represents the wants, the faculties and the feelings of one people, represent those of another people under totally different conditions'.[17] Hence all our attempts at revivals have 'signally failed' and 'the universal thirst' for a style 'in harmony with our institutions and modes of thought' cannot be denied and 'must ultimately be satisfied'.[18] To satisfy it 'principles and not results' of the arts in the past must be heeded.[19] What are these permanent principles of design to which industrial art of the nineteenth century must return? First of all, every object 'to afford perfect pleasure must be fit for the purpose and true in its construction'.[20] Its ornamentation must be related 'to the process by which (it) is to be executed'[21] and to the position in which it is to be seen. Thus a wallpaper made to cover a wall must give an 'impression of flatness.'[22]

14

The same principle applies to floor coverings.[23] Moreover, 'a carpet, whilst it covers the floor, is also the ground from which all the furniture... are, as it were, to arise: it should therefore be treated as a flat surface and have none of those imitations of raised forms and solid architectural ornaments so often seen'.[24] There must be no 'Louis Quatorze scrolls, gigantic tropical plants, shewn in high relief, and suggestive of anything but a level or plane'.[25]

To see how Digby Wyatt had devoured and digested all these theories, we must look at what he said in a lecture of 1852 called *An Attempt to define the Principles which should determine Form in the Decorative Arts*.[26] In nature 'form is, in every case, if not dependent on, at least coincident with, structural fitness'. 'Ornament appears the offspring of necessity alone.' 'Without due attention to simplicity, fitness has never been adequately carried out.'[27] In designing an object we have to be fully aware of 'all essential particulars concerning its material, its method of construction, and its uses'. Exactly the same is true of designing a building. Here also consideration of its purpose must come first and all materials must be used 'according to their nature'.

Now this insistence on truth in architecture, 'plain and manly truth' had been preached three years before Wyatt's lecture, by a man in no way connected with the Cole circle, in a book called *The Seven Lamps of Architecture*. One of the seven lamps is the Lamp of Truth, and Ruskin, in the enthusiasm of his thirty years—he was just one year older than Wyatt—thundered against 'architectural deceits' consisting of 'a mode of structure or support, other than the true one' and the endeavour to make surfaces 'represent some other material than that of which they actually consist'.[28]

Wyatt knew the *Seven Lamps* of course and even reviewed it in 1849 in the *Journal of Design*.[29] He was impressed by 'this thoughtful and eloquent book' and its 'denunciation of shams', which corresponded so well to what the *Journal of Design* had established as one of its own functions. But he was critical of other aspects of Ruskin's preaching, and here we are watching the beginnings of a conflict which is of high interest to us here, not only because it happens to be one between the future first Cambridge and the future first Oxford Slade Professors, but also because the two positions held by the two men are still of great significance for our own day.

The points of disagreement were chiefly two. One seems at first quite a small point, but is psychologically interesting enough: the attitude of Wyatt and Ruskin to their predecessor,

16

Augustus Welby Pugin, the other concerns the much wider issue of the possibility of a genuine style of modern architecture in the nineteenth century. As regards Pugin, Wyatt in a somewhat later review of Ruskin's *Stones of Venice*,[30] blamed Ruskin for his attack on Pugin and for concealing the influence which Pugin had evidently had on him.[31] And it is indeed true that Pugin, who after a hectic life of only forty years, died insane in 1852, was the fountain-head of all the reform movements in design and architecture during the nineteenth century. In his writings of 1836 and 1841, besides establishing fanatically that to build in the Gothic style only was a matter of orthodoxy and a point of honour, he also insisted that 'the great test of architectural beauty is the fitness of the design to the purpose for which it is intended',[32] that 'construction...should vary with the material employed',[33] and that it is thus absurd in wall-papers to repeat ' a perspective over a large surface ' and in carpets to use 'highly relieved foliage'.[34]

Wyatt, an honest man, felt strongly that Ruskin should have done what he himself did,[35] namely, paid 'a humble tribute to the truth and justice' of many of the propositions put forward by that 'most earnest and earliest' amongst reformers, 'the late Augustus Welby Pugin'.[36] Wyatt's charge against Ruskin is, in my opinion, only too well

17

justified, and to have recognized the questionable personal character of Ruskin at so early a date is a sign of considerable shrewdness in Wyatt. Equally shrewd is his criticism of Ruskin's 'half-views' on the problem of architecture and design under nineteenth-century conditions. This is what he writes[37]—and he was, I think, the first to recognize this valid objection to Ruskin as well as Morris:

Instead of boldly recognising the tendencies of the age, which are inevitable...instead of considering the means of improving these tendencies... he either puts up his back against their further development, or would attempt to bring back the world of art to what its course of action was four centuries ago. Our course in this nineteenth century may be hateful, if you please; denounce it, but as it *is* our course, wise men should recognise the fact.

The inadequacy of Ruskin's argument, says Wyatt, comes out most clearly in his lack of a 'consistent theory of mechanical repetition as applied to art', that is of machine-art and in his 'very lop-sided view of railways and railway-architecture'. And it is true that in the *Seven Lamps* Ruskin lists 'machine-made ornament of any kind' amongst the architectural deceits, and owing to his almost exclusive concern with ornamentation as the source of architectural beauty[38] never considers the aesthetic possibilities of

18

machine-shaped forms. And as regards railway-architecture, that is the new architecture of iron and glass, Ruskin was indeed at first painfully confused and then bluntly hostile. In the *Seven Lamps* he says on the one hand—a unique remark, I think, in his vast *œuvre*—that 'the time is probably near when a new system of architectural laws will be developed, entirely adapted to metallic construction',[39] but on the other hand, he calls 'the iron roofs and pillars of our railway stations... not architecture at all'.[40]

Wyatt, in his turn, wrote an article in the *Journal of Design* which he called *Principles and Treatment of Ironwork*[41] and which contains a juster appreciation of the architectural values of metal structures—and an appreciation moreover which must be amongst the earliest and most generous.[42] Here is what he wrote; 'It has become', he says, 'difficult to define where civil engineering ends and architecture begins.' Bridges such as the tubular Britannia Bridge across the Menai Straits and the Conway Suspension Bridge are amongst the 'wonders of the world', and as for Isambard Kingdom Brunel, the designer of the Clifton and Hungerford Bridges and Wyatt's fellow-designer later on at Paddington Station, 'his independence of meretricious and adventitious ornament is as great and as above prejudice as his

19

engineering works are daring in conception and masterly in execution. From such beginnings', Wyatt continues, 'what glories may be in reserve, when England has systematized a scale of form and proportion—a vocabulary of its own, in which to speak to the world the language of its power, and freedom of thought and feeling, we may trust ourselves to dream, but we dare not predict. Whatever the result may be,' he concludes, 'it is impossible to disregard the fact, that the building for the Exhibition of 1851 is likely to accelerate the "consummation devoutly to be wished" and that the novelty of its form and details will be likely to exercise a powerful influence upon national taste'.[43]

When Wyatt wrote this manifesto—a document not, I think, hitherto known and yet of just as much importance in the history of taste as the *Seven Lamps*—he was already secretary to the Exhibition, and Paxton's design for the Crystal Palace had been made, approved and published.[44]

And so we come to the Crystal Palace, acclaimed by some, attacked by others, the thrill of the common man, including Thackeray,[45] and the *bête noire* of Ruskin. Here again, from the vantage point of to-day, there can be no question that Wyatt was right and that Ruskin was wrong. Wyatt in a factual and restrained address to the Institution of Civil Engineers in 1851,[46] said that the Crystal

Palace 'may be expected to produce, hereafter, important changes in the construction and appearance of many extensive buildings throughout the country'—which is exactly what has happened, though only fifty, sixty, seventy years after the event. Ruskin hurried an appendix (no. 17) into his *Stones of Venice*, just in time for its publication in 1851, to state that iron and glass are 'eternally separated from all good and great things by a gulf which not all the tubular bridges nor engineering of ten thousand nineteenth centuries cast into one great bronze-foreheaded century will ever overpass one inch of'. He felt so strongly about it that even his style went wrong. And he did not hesitate to make it clear what specific building had occasioned this outburst:

The quality of bodily industry which the Crystal Palace expresses, is very great. So far it is good. The quantity of thought it expresses is, I suppose, a single and admirable thought...probably not a bit brighter than thousands of thoughts which pass through (its designer's) active and intelligent brain every hour—that it might be possible to build a greenhouse larger than ever greenhouse was built before. This thought and some very ordinary algebra are as much as all that glass can represent of human intellect.[47]

And Ruskin was so convinced of the truth and urgency of this protest that he went on making it whenever he could find an opportunity. When the Crystal Palace had been re-erected at Sydenham in 1854 (with Wyatt's various courts inside) he wrote a special pamphlet in which he deplores that after 300 years 'of the most curious investigation' all that architecture has been able to produce for this 'national museum' is a 'magnified conservatory',[48] and in *Praeterita* again he refers to the Crystal Palace as to a 'cucumber frame'.[49]

So, to say it again, in respect of contemporary architecture and industrial design, Cambridge undeniably scores. However, I know only too well that it would be unwise for me from this chair to carry too far specific comparisons between the first Cambridge and the first Oxford Slade Professor. For Ruskin, though perhaps more often wrong than Wyatt, and though no doubt the less acceptable character, was a man of genius, and Wyatt was not. Ruskin was, moreover, of burning eloquence and high sensitivity, and in both these qualities Wyatt was somewhat defective. We need only compare a few passages referring to painting and architecture. Here is first as much as Wyatt in his Slade course does in the way of analysing a Giotto or Giottesque painting, the *Marriage of Saint Francis with Poverty* at Assisi: 'A vivid and graceful embodiment of that incident.'[50] And here

22

is Ruskin on Giotto's *Meeting at the Golden Gate* in the Arena Chapel at Padua.[51]

It is [he writes] full of the most solemn grace and tenderness. The face of Anna, half seen, is most touching in its depth of expression, and it is very interesting to observe how Giotto has enhanced its sweetness by giving a harder and grosser character than is usual with him to the heads of the other two principal female figures, and by the rough and weather-beaten countenance of the entering shepherd.

And now, secondly, here is a typical Ruskin remark on the nature of the Gothic style in architecture:[52]

The feelings and habits in the workman [he writes] must be understood. There is first the habit of hard and rapid working; the industry of the tribes of the North, quickened by the coldness of the climate, and giving an expression of sharp energy to all they do, as opposed to the languor of the Southern tribes.

Again, as a criterion of good Gothic work the following[53] could hardly have been improved even by the late Professor Prior, the best English interpreter of the Gothic style:

See if it looks as if it had been built by strong men; if it has the sort of roughness, and largeness, and nonchalance, mixed in places with the exquisite tenderness which seems always to be a sign-manual of the broad vision, and massy power of men who can see past the work they are doing, and

23

betray here and there something like disdain for it. If the building has that character, it is much already in its favour; it will go hard but it proves a noble one.

Partiality forbids me to match this with a detailed quotation from Wyatt's Slade lectures on the history of architecture with their rare dim remarks about 'a lighter scale of parts', or 'a beauty of refinement in the execution of foliage (and) mouldings'.[54]

However, perhaps one should not be shocked by this deficiency in our Wyatt. For since all his signal contributions concern the principles of design and the appreciation of a new technological architecture, why should he be expected to have been a man of any special sensibility? Here also lies, of course, the explanation of the fact how so undeniably remarkable a man can have been so undeniably bad an architect. Such a contrast between theory and performance is frequent amongst Victorian architects. You find it in Pugin and Gilbert Scott, even more blatantly in Viollet-le-Duc, and in many others.

Very generally speaking one can perhaps say that harmony between theory and performance must be rooted in a much deeper harmony between thought and feeling.[55] This harmony returned only into the arts of design with William Morris. Morris, it is known, appreciated Owen Jones;

24

Wyatt he will hardly have noticed much. The man to whom he owed most was Ruskin. From Ruskin he received his romantic backward-looking enthusiasm for the Middle Ages. From Ruskin he received his faith in art as 'a happiness for the maker and for the user',[56] and from Ruskin his hatred against his own century, its machines, its commerce and its grimy cities.

Wyatt would have approved no more of Morris than he did of Ruskin. Wyatt worshipped industry and 'the comparative annihilation of time and space, through the railway and telegraph'. He firmly believed in 'free trade...free press, free navigation, free education...comparatively free postal communication' and 'that ruthless destroyer of conventional restrictions—Competition'.[57]

Who in listening to this would not be reminded of Prince Albert's unforgettable address at the Lord Mayor's Banquet of 21 March 1850, in which he undertook to interest the City in his exhibition. In this address, more than in any other document known to me, that triumphant optimism of the mid-nineteenth century stands out, which it is so difficult for us in our troubled scepticism and disillusion to grasp.

Nobody [Prince Albert said] who has paid any attention to the peculiar features of our present era, will doubt for a moment that we are living at a period of most wonderful transition, which tends rapidly to accomplish that great end, to which, indeed, all history points—the realisation of the unity of mankind....The distances which separated the different nations and parts of the globe are rapidly vanishing before the achievements of modern inventions, and we can traverse them with incredible ease....On the other hand, the great principle of division of labour, which may be called the moving power of civilisation, is being extended to all branches of science, industry and art. Whilst formerly the greatest mental energies strove at universal knowledge, and that knowledge was confined to the few, now they are directed on specialities...but the knowledge acquired becomes at once the property of the community at large. The products of all quarters of the globe are placed at our disposal, and we have only to choose which is the best and the cheapest for our purposes, and the powers of production are entrusted to the stimulus of competition and capital. So man is approaching a more complete fulfilment of that great and sacred mission which he has to perform in this world....I confidently hope that the first impression which the view of this vast collection will produce upon the spectator will be that of deep thankfulness to the Almighty for the blessings He has bestowed upon us already here below.[58]

Well—evidently, in spite of the influence which Pugin and the German Romantics who had preceded him had exerted on Albert and Wyatt and the others of the Henry Cole circle, Albert's Almighty was very different from Pugin's. And consequently, although Pugin was right through his life a passionate student of Christian design of the past and a most fertile designer himself, he never took an interest in such things as schools of design, museums of design, and so on.[59] Prince Albert and the Cole circle, on the other hand, are memorable as the instigators and first administrators of Government Schools of Design, of exhibitions, of the establishment of museums, such as the Victoria and Albert Museum, of State-endowed competitions for artists—in short—to quote once again the venerable past-Master of Trinity, the Rev. William Whewell—of art 'not to gratify the tastes of the few, (but) to supply the wants of the many'.[60]

Morris, you will at once see, could have said exactly the same, and did say almost the same: 'What business have we with art at all, unless all can share it?'[61] But he meant, of course, something utterly different. Morris's aim was, to repeat it once more, to make all work and all art a joy for the maker and the user. To Cole and the others the aim is, as Wyatt put it in 1849, to provide 'the enjoyments of taste to the enormous and now all-powerful Bourgeois class'.[62] I will not dwell on the

27

class aspects of this. What matters to me is that Wyatt thinks of the industrialist and the designer for industry, not of the workman. Morris despised the designer for industry. This is what he has to say about him and the position in which he will be in the mildly reformed society wished for by certain benevolent people. The passage is far too little known:

A highly gifted and carefully educated man shall...squint at a sheet of paper, and the results of that squint shall set a vast number of well-fed, contented operatives...turning crank-handles for ten hours a day, bidding them keep what gifts and education they may have been born with for their—I was going to say leisure hours, but I don't know how to, for if I were to work ten hours a day at work I despised and hated, I should spend my leisure, I·hope, in political agitation, but I fear— in drinking.... Well, from this system are to come threefold blessings—food and clothing, poorish lodgings and a little leisure to the operatives, enormous riches to the capitalists that rent them, together with moderate riches to the squinter on the paper; and lastly, very decidedly lastly, abundance of cheap art for the operatives and crank-turners to buy.[63]

Now Cole's, and to a certain extent Wyatt's, aim in life was just that cheap art for everybody. Hence Cole's art manufactures of the 'forties, hence his activities as Secretary to the Department

28

of Practical Art, and later as Director of the Victoria and Albert Museum, and hence Redgrave's job as Inspector General of Art.

Looking at it from the point of view of to-day, Wyatt, Cole, Redgrave are the predecessors of our Councils of Industrial Design and Art Councils and all the other governmentally—and perhaps academically—aided means of promoting art. They were just as convinced as we are, and as Morris was, that not all is well in the realm of art and architecture, but they believed that by better training and by lecturing and exhibiting, art, architecture and aesthetic understanding might be re-established within our own society, whereas Morris believed that a complete change of heart, if not a complete upheaval of society, would have to precede the re-establishment of an art worth having.

Who in this argument is right? We have to ask ourselves just as urgently now as they had to in 1851. Who is right? Ruskin and his disciple Morris, or Digby Wyatt?

In asking this question in this form, I have cunningly placed Wyatt on the same level as Ruskin and Morris. If you are ready, after having listened to me, to be taken in by this, I shall have succeeded in my humble intention of making the first Cambridge Slade Professor appear for an hour more interesting than he really was.

APPENDIX A

LIST OF WYATT'S WRITINGS

[The following list of Wyatt's writings is from the catalogues of the British Museum, the Royal Institute of British Architects, the Victoria and Albert Museum, and from the obituary notice in *The British Architect*, vol. VII.]

On the Art of the Mosaic, Ancient and Modern.
  Trans. Soc. of Arts, 1847.

Mosaics as Applied to Architectural Decoration.
  Sess. Papers, R.I.B.A., 1847.

Specimens of Geometrical Mosaic of the Middle Ages.
  London, 1848.

A Report on the Eleventh French Exposition of the Products of Industry. London, 1849.

Further Report made to H.R.H. Prince Albert...of Preliminary Enquiries into the Willingness of Manufacturers and Others to Support Periodical Exhibitions of the Works of Industry of all Nations. London, 1849.

Observations on Polychromatic Decoration in Italy. MS.
  R.I.B.A., 1850.

The Exhibition under its Commercial Aspects.
  Journal of Design and Manufactures, vol. V, 1851.

On the Construction of the Building for the Exhibition...
  in 1851. *Proc. Inst. Civ. Engineers*, vol. X, 1851 (also in the *Official Catalogue* of the Exhibition, London, 1851).

The Industrial Arts of the Nineteenth Century. Fol., London, 1851–3.

An Attempt to Define the Principles which should determine Form in the Decorative Arts. *Lectures on the Results of the Great Exhibition.* London, 1852

Specimens of Ornamental Art Workmanship in Gold, Silver, Iron, Brass and Bronze. Fol., London, 1852.

Metalwork and its Artistic Design. Fol., London, 1852.

A. A. P. C. Blanc, *The History of the Painters of all Nations,* ed. M. D. Wyatt. London, 1852.

Remarks on G. Abbati's Paper on Pompeian Decorations. *Sess. Papers, R.I.B.A.*, 1853.

The Byzantine and Romanesque Courts in the Crystal Palace (with J. B. Waring). London, 1854.

The Italian Court in the Crystal Palace (with J. B. Waring). London, 1854.

The Medieval Court in the Crystal Palace (with J. B. Waring). London, 1854.

The Renaissance Court in the Crystal Palace (with J. B. Waring). London, 1854.

Views of the Crystal Palace (1st ser.). London, 1854.

An Address delivered in the Crystal Palace at the opening of an Exhibition of Works of Art belonging to the Arundel Society. London, 1855.

Mosaics...of Sta Sophia at Constantinople. *Sess. Papers, R.I.B.A.*, 1865.

Observations on Renaissance and Italian Ornament (in O. Jones, *The Grammar of Ornament*). Fol., London, 1856.

Paris Universal Exhibition; Report on Furniture and Decorations. London, 1856.

Notices of Sculpture in Ivory (Arundel Society). London, 1856.

Notice of the late John Britton. *Sess. Papers, R.I.B.A.*, 1857.

The Sacred Grotto of St Benedict at Subiaco.
Sess. Papers, R.I.B.A., 1857.

Specimens of Geometrical Mosaics manufactured by Maw and Co. Fol., London, 1857.

On the Principles of Design applicable to Textile Art (in J. B. Waring, *The Art Treasures of the United Kingdom*). London, 1857–8.

Observations on Metallic Art (in J. B. Waring, *The Art Treasures of the United Kingdom*). London, 1857–8.

Influence Exercised on Ceramic Manufactures by the late Herbert Minton. London, 1858.

Early Habitations of the Irish, and especially the Cramoges of Lake Castles. *Sess. Papers, R.I.B.A.*, 1858.

On the Architectural Career of Sir Charles Barry. *Sess. Papers, R.I.B.A.*, 1859–60.

Illuminated Manuscripts as Illustrative of the Arts of Design. London, 1860.

The Art of Illuminating (with W. R. Tymms). London, 1860.

What Illuminating Was. London, 1861.

On the Present Aspect of the Fine and Decorative Arts in Italy. *Journal Soc. of Arts*, 1862.

The Loan Collection at South Kensington. *Fine Arts Quart. Rev.*, vols. I and II, 1863.

On Pictorial Mosaic as an Architectural Embellishment. *Sess. Papers, R.I.B.A.*, 1866.

A Report to Accompany the Designs for a National Gallery. London, 1866.

The Relations which should exist between Architecture and the Industrial Arts. *Architectural Association*, London, *c.* 1867.

On the Foreign Artists employed in England during the Sixteenth Century. *Sess. Papers, R.I.B.A.*, 1868.

The History of the Manufacture of Clocks. London, 1868.

Report on the Art of Decoration at the International Exhibition. Paris, 1867; London, 1868.

Introduction and Notes on Examples of Decorative Design, Selected from Drawings of Italian Masters in the Uffizi at Florence. Pamphlet, London, 1869.

Fine Art; its History, Theory, Practice. (Slade Lectures at Cambridge.) London and New York, 1870.

Report on Miscellaneous Paintings, London International Exhibition, 1871. Pamphlet, London, 1871.

An Architect's Notebook in Spain. London, 1872.

On the Most Characteristic Features of the Buildings of the Vienna Exhibition of 1873. London, 1874.

The Utrecht Psalter; Reports on the Age of the Manuscript. (By Sir M. D. Wyatt and others.) Fol., London, 1874.

APPENDIX B

LIST OF WYATT'S ARCHITECTURAL AND OTHER WORKS

(a) Works Illustrated in Journals or Mentioned on Obituary Notices

Pompeian, Byzantine, English Gothic, Italian, Renaissance Courts, etc. (see p. 38, n. 7) at the Crystal Palace, 1854. *The Builder*, vol. XII.

Paddington Station, London (with Brunel as engineer), 1854–5. *The Builder*, vol. XII.

Prize in Competition for Cavalry Barracks, Woolwich (with T. H. Wyatt), 1855.

Interior of Chancel, North Marston Church, Bucks (Memorial to J. Camden Neild, for Queen Victoria), 1855. *Illus. Lond. News*, Sept. 1855.

Royal Engineers' Crimean War Memorial, Chatham (Entrance to the School of Military Engineering, Brompton Barracks), 1861. *The Builder*, vol. XIX.

Indian Government Store, Belvedere Road, Lambeth, London, 1861–4 (demolished).

Designs for the Albert Memorial. (Unexecuted. According to *The Builder*, vol. XXI, p. 233, Wyatt sent in three designs, one for an open four-porticoed classical temple for the statue of the Prince, and other statues, one for a cross in the Italian Gothic style; and one more purely sculptural with the seated figure of the Prince crowned by Fame.)

Garrison Church, Woolwich (with T. H. Wyatt), 1862. *The Builder*, vol. XXI and *Illus. Lond. News*, Jan. 1863.

Office Building, Grafton Street, Dublin, 1863.
  The Builder, vol. XXI.

Saloon and Fernery, Ashridge, Herts, 1864. Drawings for
  the Fernery at R.I.B.A.; cf. p. 38, n. 7.

Addenbrooke's Hospital, Cambridge, 1864–5 (extensions,
  including new west front).

Rothschild Mausoleum, West Ham Cemetery, probably
  1867 (Mrs Rothschild died in December 1866).

India Office, London, Inner Courtyard, 1867.
  The Builder, vol. XXV; *Building News, Lond.*, vol. XVI.

Castle Ashby, Northants, Garden Gates.
  The Builder, vol. XXVI, 1868. (See also under (b).)

Possingworth Manor, Sussex, 1868. For L. Huth.
  The Builder, vol. XXVI; *The Architect*, vol. I.

Clare College, Cambridge, 1870–2 (restoration of Hall and
  Combination Room).

R. Indian Civil Engineers' College, Coopers Hill, Surrey
  (now Training College), founded 1871.

Alford House, Kensington, London. Drawings exhibited
  at the Royal Academy, 1872.

Offices for Lloyd's, Gracechurch Street, London, 1877.
  The Builder, vol. XXXV.

(b) OTHER ARCHITECTURAL WORK

Azores: Mansion.

Burma: work at Rangoon.

Essex: Barracks, Chapel and Hospital for the East India
  Company at Warley.

Glamorgan: The Ham.

Hampshire: Brambridge House. (Reconstruction and
  redecoration for Sir Thomas Fairbairn, illustrated in
  the sale catalogue of J. D. Wood and Co., 14 Sept.
  1949.)

India: Post Office at Calcutta.

London: (i) Adelphi Theatre (with T. H. Wyatt); (ii) Burlington Fine Arts Club; (iii) East India Museum (perhaps adaptation of Elm Grove, now demolished); (iv) 12 Kensington Palace Gardens (reconstruction and redecoration of house for Alexander Collie, between 1865 and 1875); (v) Oxford Street, offices for Purdey and Cowlan; (vi) Piccadilly, Conservatory and Saloon, Northampton House.

Middlesex: Indian Lunatic Asylum at Ealing.

Northants: Castle Ashby, Conservatory, etc. (See also under (a).)

Prince Edward Island: varied work.

Surrey: (i) a house at Caterham; (ii) Newells, near Horsham; (iii) The Mount at Norbury Hill (?), called Norwood in the obituaries.

Sussex: (i) Old Lands; (ii) a house at Uckfield.

(c) Restorations

Compton Winyates.

Isfield Park, Sussex.

(d) Designs

Executed for Messrs Woollam (wall-papers). Maw (tiles, 1861). Templeton (carpets). Hurell James and Co., and others.

NOTES

1 Matthew Digby Wyatt was born at Rowde, near Devizes, in 1820, died in 1877, and was buried at Usk in Monmouthshire. His father was a barrister in Ireland. He was articled to his brother, Thomas Henry (1807–80), travelled in France, Germany and Italy in 1844–6, and became Surveyor to the East India Company in 1855. Other dates and events are mentioned in the text of the lecture.

2 Sir Henry Cole: *Fifty Years of Public Work* (London, 1884). See also the Cole Papers at the Victoria and Albert Museum.

3 The General Bearing of the Great Exhibition on the Progress of Art and Science in *Lectures on the Results of the Great Exhibition of* 1851, p. 1. (London, 1852.)

4 Sir Henry Cole, *loc. cit.*, vol. I, p. 105.

5 Semper stayed in England from 1850 to 1853. He designed the Canadian, Egyptian, Danish and Swedish exhibits at the Great Exhibition and was made a member of the teaching staff of the Department of Practical Art in 1851. The *Journal of Design* reprinted a paper of his on polychromy, vol. VI, pp. 112 et seq. At the Victoria and Albert Museum is a manuscript *Practical Art in Metals and Hard Materials: On Collections, their History*, etc., by him. The chief outcome of his stay was the pamphlet *Wissenschaft, Industrie und Kunst* (Braunschweig 1852), the outcome, he writes, of a private demand for a report. Was it asked for by Prince Albert? Or by Cole? On Semper and Redgrave see L. Ettlinger, in *Journal of the Warburg and Courtauld Institutes*, vol. III (1939–40).

6 The problem of literature is more complex; for here we find some of the greatest at the same time amongst those

37

most successful with the public. However, if one remembers that the most characteristic form of literature in the nineteenth century is the novel, it will be patent why a certain harmony between the artist and the public was quite possible. The novel in the hands of Balzac, or Zola, or Flaubert, or Dickens, or Thackeray, or Hardy, or James, or Tolstoi, or Dostoyevski was descriptive and factual and often even scientific enough to please.

7 Victoria and Albert Museum V. 1, and Box 85. They also contain Wyatt's water-colours for the German Medieval Vestibule, the English Medieval Vestibule, the English Medieval Court, the French and Italian Medieval Vestibule, the Renaissance, Elizabethan and Italian Courts and the Italian Vestibule. That these water-colours are by Wyatt's hand is borne out by a water-colour of S. Benedetto at Subiaco at the Royal Institute of British Architects which also owns a set of plans, elevations, sections and perspectives for the Fern-House at Ashridge, and a timid drawing of a Gothic window, dated 1848 (and probably by a lesser Wyatt). At the Victoria and Albert Museum in addition (C. 124) designs for roofing-tiles for Messrs Maw.

8 Among sources of the motif of the continuous, round-headed arcade on short piers with foliated capitals, which was so very popular for mid-nineteenth century town premises is, for example, the Bargello courtyard in Florence.

9 Vol. IV, 1850–1, pp. 10, et seq. The article is not signed but Wyatt's authorship is proved by the text to his *Specimens of Ornamental Art Workmanship in Gold, Silver, Iron, Brass and Bronze* (London, 1852).

10 His editorship is revealed in a pencilled note at the foot of the preface to the Victoria and Albert Museum copy of vol. VI.

11 Redgrave was born in 1804, Dyce in 1806, Cole in 1808, Owen Jones in 1809 and Semper in 1803.

12 There is no adequate exposition of the *Journal of Design*, yet Dr Giedion (to whom little escapes) has recently drawn attention to it in *Mechanization Takes Command* (New York 1949), pp. 350 et seq., and I have briefly dealt with Owen Jones and Semper in *Academies of Art, Past and Present* (Camb. Univ. Press 1941); also in *The Architectural Review*, vol. LXXXI, 1937.

13 *Pioneers of Modern Design; From William Morris to Walter Gropius* (New York, 1949).

14 O. Jones, *The True and the False in the Decorative Arts*, London, 1863 (Lectures given at the School of Practical Art in 1852), p. 14. Cf. Morris, 'The Decorative Arts are in a state of anarchy and disorganisation' (*The Lesser Arts*, 1877; *Coll. Works*, vol. XXII, p. 9).

15 *Journal of Design*, vol. II (1849–50), p. 17. Morris: 'We, if no age else, have learnt the trick of masquerading in other men's cast-off clothes' (*Coll. Works*, vol. XXII, p. 315).

16 G. Semper, *Wissenschaft, Industrie und Kunst*, p. 11 (Braunschweig, 1852).

17 O. Jones, *loc. cit.*, p. 8. Morris on the Gothic Revivalists of the mid-nineteenth century: 'They... thought it could be artificially replanted in a society totally different from that which gave birth to it' (*Coll. Works*, vol. XXII, p. 319).

18 O. Jones in *Journal of Design*, vol. V (1851), p. 90.

19 O. Jones, *The True and the False*, p. 39.

20 Ibid. p. 14. Cf. Morris: '...the necessary and essential beauty which arises out of the fitness of a piece of craftsmanship for the use (for) which it is made'. (Quoted from May Morris, *W. M., Artist, Writer, Socialist*, Oxford, 1936, vol. I, p. 317. The quotation comes from a paper *The Ideal Book*, read in 1893. Stanley Morison drew my attention to it.)

21 W. Dyce in *Journal of Design*, vol. I (1849), p. 93.

22 *Journal of Design*, vol. I (1849), p. 80. Cf. Morris: 'As to paperhangings . . . the more mechanical the process, the less direct should be the imitation of natural forms' (*Coll. Works*, vol. XXII, p. 190).

23 W. Dyce in *Journal of Design*, vol. I (1849), pp. 91 et seq.

24 R. Redgrave in *Journal of Design*, vol. IV (1850–1), p. 15. Cf. Morris: 'As for a carpet design, it seems quite clear that it should be quite flat, that it should give no more . . . than the merest hint of one plane behind another' (*Coll. Works*, vol. XXII, p. 195).

25 *Journal of Design*, vol. III (1850), p. 175.

26 One of the *Lectures on the Results of the Great Exhibition* arranged by the Society of Arts (cf. p. 31). Wyatt's lecture was given on 21 April 1852.

27 Morris: 'Simplicity is the foundation of all worthy art' (*Coll. Works*, vol. XXII, p. 294).

28 *The Lamp of Truth*, Lib. Edit., vol. VIII, p. 60.

29 Vol. II, 1849–50, pp. 72 et seq. My attribution of the unsigned review is based on the identity of points of view with those in the later article referred to on p. 42, n. 35.

30 Vol. VI (1851–2), pp. 25 et seq.

31 Ruskin wrote (App. 12 to vol. I, Lib. Edit. vol. IX, pp. 436–9) that Pugin 'is not a great architect, but one of the smallest possible or conceivable architects' and links up that hysterical statement with equally hysterical ones against the 'miserable influence' of Romanism, the 'fatuity, self-inflicted and the stubbornness in resistance to God's Word' which characterizes the Catholic. 'No imbecility', he goes on, 'so absolute, no treachery so contemptible' as theirs. Later on, in 1856, he defended himself explicitly against ever having in the least been influenced by Pugin (Lib. Edit., vol. V, pp. 428 et seq.): 'I glanced at Pugin's Contrasts once, in the Oxford archi-

tectural reading room, during an idle forenoon. His Remarks on Articles in *The Rambler* (1850) were brought under my notice by some of the reviews. I never read a word of any other of his works, not feeling, from the style of his architecture, the smallest interest in his opinion.' One would be readier to believe Ruskin if it were not for such facts as the complete omission of his married life from *Praeterita*.

32 *Contrasts* (1836), p. 1.

33 *The True Principles of Printed or Christian Architecture* (1841), p. 1.

34 *The True Principles*, pp. 25 and 26. The position of Pugin in the history of architectural and art criticism is in fact much more complex than it must appear here. I have brought together some more passages of importance in a florilegium in *The Architectural Review*, vol. xciv, 1943. For an excellent summing up see Sir Kenneth Clark, *The Gothic Revival* (London, 1928). Briefly what happened was this. In Pugin, owing to his newly acquired catholic zeal, the earlier aesthetic teachings of such romantic converts as Friedrich von Schlegel were revived and applied specifically to architecture and design. Schlegel (*Europa*, 1803, vol. ii, pt. ii, pp. 143–5) said: 'Vergeblich sucht ihr die Malerkunst wieder hervorzurufen, wenn nicht erst Religion oder philosophische Mystik wenigstens die Idee derselben wieder hervorgerufen hat.' Pugin said that churches of any, including architectural, value 'can only be produced...by...men who were thoroughly imbued with devotion for, and faith in, the religion for whose worship they were erected' (*Contrasts*, p. 2). This religious foundation gave a new twist to the *bienséance* and *convenance* of the classic French architectural theory of the seventeenth and eighteenth centuries. To consider utility now became not a matter of common sense but of truthfulness. Cole, Owen Jones and Wyatt took over the utilitarian theses without bothering about their philo-

sophical premisses, the Gothic Revival architects (notably Gilbert Scott, who in his *Remarks on Secular and Domestic Architecture* (London, 1858), p. 241, praised Pugin as 'the great reformer of architecture') took over the exclusive faith in Gothic form and the substructure of the system of which to Pugin it was the necessary expression, while Ruskin and then Morris took over the whole system but without its religious foundation. They agreed with Pugin (and the earlier Romantics—from Herder and young Goethe, and from Edward Young onwards) that art and architecture express the state of mind and feeling of a man and a society, but they did not draw the narrow conclusion that only a restoration of medieval Christianity could restore the arts. Still, their own vaguer medievalist sociology was perhaps no more real.

35   *Journal of Design*, vol. IV (1850–1), p. 75.

36   Cf. also *Fine Art* (London and New York, 1870), p. 75.

37   *Journal of Design*, vol. II (1849–50), p. 72.

38   'Ornamentation is the principal part of architecture', *Architecture and Painting* (1853), Addenda to Lectures I and II, Lib. Edit., vol. XII, p. 88.

39   *The Lamp of Truth*, Lib. Edit., vol. VIII, p. 66.

40   Ibid. p. 67.

41   Vol. IV, pp. 10 et seq. and pp. 74 et seq. A passage from this article has already been quoted on p. 13, see p. 38, n. 9.

42   See my *Pioneers of Modern Design*, loc. cit. pp. 68 et seq.

43   In praise of iron and glass still a little earlier (and not mentioned either in Sigfried Giedion's *Space, Time and Architecture* or my *Pioneers of Modern Design*) is *Journal of Design*, vol. II (1849–50), p. 148, on Bunning's Coal Exchange (illustrated by Henry-Russell Hitchcock in *The*

Architectural Review, vol. CI, 1947): 'We have a structure which manifests at once that the architect very properly made its purpose and destination the first and ruling thought.... Mr Bunning has successfully employed iron and glass abundantly, usefully and ornamentally.' Again an article on *The Prospect of Iron and Glass Edifices* came out in vol. VI (1851–2), pp. 16 et seq. Here we read: 'The novel union as building materials necessitates a new treatment, and we have our hopes will produce a new era in architecture'.

44   See, for example, *Journal of Design*, vol. III (August 1850), p. 190.

45   'A blazing arch of lucid glass
         Leaps like a fountain from the grass
         A rare pavilion such as man
         Saw never since mankind began.'

46   *Proc. Inst. Civ. Eng.* vol. X (14 January 1851), p. 133.

47   Lib. Edit., vol. III, p. 456.

48   Lib. Edit., vol. XII, pp. 418–19.

49   Lib. Edit., vol. XXXV, p. 47.

50   *Fine Art*, loc. cit. p. 243.

51   *Giotto and his Works*...(1853–60), Lib. Edit., vol. XXIV, p. 58.

52   *The Stones of Venice*, vol. II (1853), Lib. Edit., vol. X, p. 240.

53   Ibid. p. 268.

54   *Fine Art*, loc. cit., pp. 49–51.

55   Cf. the all-pervading emphasis placed on the lack of balance between thought and feeling during the nineteenth century in both Dr Giedion's monumental books, *Space, Time and Architecture*, and *Mechanization takes Command*.

56   See, for example, in *The Lamp of Life*: 'So long as men work *as* men putting their heart into what they do...

48

there will be that in the handling which is above all price,
(Lib. Edit., vol. VIII, p. 214), and even more clearly: 'The
right question to ask, respecting all ornament, is simply
this: Was it done with enjoyment—was the carver happy,
while he was about it?' (Lib. Edit., vol. VIII, p. 218). It is
from this point of view also that Ruskin had to condemn
the Crystal Palace and railway stations. There are indeed
no happy craftsmen expected to be busy on them. But, and
here appears a fundamental fallacy, while the criterion
of the joy in making can be applied to craft—a hand-made
vase possesses certain qualities due to the touch of the
human hand which in the machine-turned vase must be
absent—it cannot be applied to much that is best in architecture, unless one is ready to confine the aesthetic values
of architecture to the values of decoration added to it, as
indeed Ruskin did—see p. 42, n. 38. But the strictly
architectural values of architecture, i.e. values of siting,
grouping, proportion, relations of solid and void, spatial
rhythm, etc., have at all times been a matter of design
largely independent of the executive hand. That is as true
of the Parthenon as of the Pantheon, of Périgeux as of the
Palazzo Pitti.

57 'The Exhibition under its Commercial Aspect',
Journal of Design, vol. V (1851), pp. 153 et seq. Morris
on competition can be read in several of his Lectures on
Socialism (*Coll. Works*, vol. XXIII); for example: 'I hold
that the condition of competition between man and man
is bestial' (p. 172).

58 *The Principal Speeches and Addresses of H.R.H. the
Prince Consort* (London, 1862), pp. 110 et seq. Compare
with this passage Sir Henry Cole's on the exhibition: 'The
history of the world, I venture to say, records no event
comparable in its promotion of human industry' (*Sir
Henry Cole*, loc. cit. vol. I, p. 116). Sir Henry Cole also said
that the exhibition had only been possible because of the
'perfect security for property, commercial freedom, and

facility of transport' existing in the world at the time (ibid., vol. II, p. 208).

59   Neither did Morris: 'Until our streets are decent and orderly, and our town gardens break the bricks and mortar every here and there . . . until the great drama of the seasons can touch our workman with other feelings than the misery of winter and the weariness of summer . . . our museums and art schools will be but amusements of the rich' (*Coll Works*, vol. XXII, p. 138). Again Pugin's religious premisses have been replaced by social, but also more broadly human, premisses.

60   Loc. cit. (see p. 37, n. 3), p. 18.

61   J. W. Mackail, *The Life of William Morris*, vol. II (London, 1899), p. 99.

62   *A Report on the Eleventh French Exposition of the Products of Industry* (London, 1849), p. 4.

63   *Making the Best of it* (Lecture of *c.* 1878–9, *Collected Works*, vol. XXII, pp. 114–15).

THE PLATES

PLATE I

MATTHEW DIGBY WYATT

from the portrait in the R.I.B.A. by Ossani (*c*. 1870)

PLATE II

Crystal Palace: The Byzantine Court

PLATE III

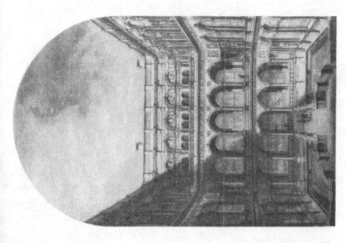

(b) Courtyard of India Office, Whitehall

(a) Office Building, Grafton Street, Dublin

PLATE IV

(*a*) Alford House, Kensington

(*b*) Addenbrooke's Hospital, Cambridge

PLATE VI

Mausoleum for Eveline Rothschild at the
Jewish Cemetery, West Ham